BASS
RECORDED VERSIONS

AEROSMITH BASS COLLECTION

CONTENTS

PHOTOGRAPHY BY MARY ELLEN MATTHEWS
MUSIC TRANSCRIPTIONS BY STEVE GORENBERG

ISBN 0-634-01647-4

HAL•LEONARD®
CORPORATION

7777 W. BLUEMOUND RD. P.O. BOX 13819 MILWAUKEE, WI 53213

Visit Hal Leonard Online at
www.halleonard.com

from *Rocks*

Back in the Saddle

Words and Music by Steven Tyler and Joe Perry

Tune down 1/2 step:
(low to high) E♭-A♭-D♭-G♭

Intro

Moderate Rock ♩ = 116

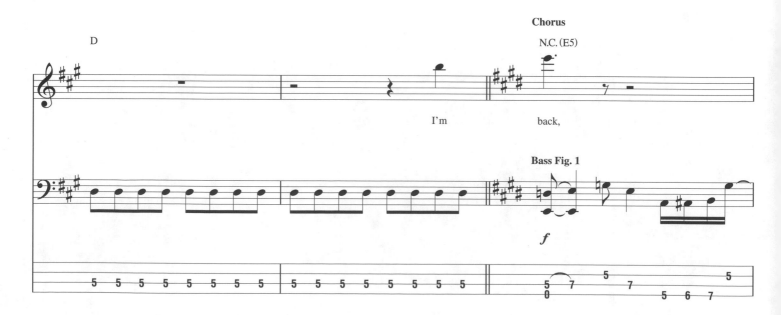

I'm back in the saddle a - gain. _____ I'm

End Bass Fig. 1

Bass: w/ Bass Fig. 1

back, I'm back in the sad - dle a - gain. _____

Verse

A   D   A   D

1. Rid - in' in - to town a - lone ___ by the light of the moon, _____

A   D

I'm look - in' for old Su - kie Jones, ___

Bass: w/ Bass Fig. 3

Fools gold out of their mine, _____ the girls are soak - in' wet. _ No tongue's dri - er than mine, _

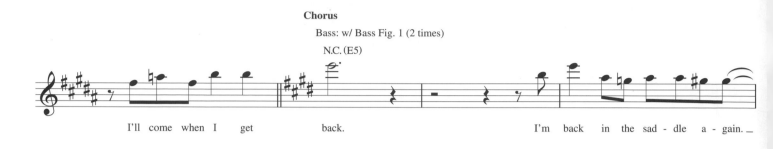

Chorus
Bass: w/ Bass Fig. 1 (2 times)
N.C. (E5)

I'll come when I get back. I'm back in the sad - dle a - gain. _

_____ I'm back, I'm back in the sad - dle a - gain. _____

Bridge
Asus4   A   Bsus4/A B/A G/A   N.C.   A5

I'm rid - in', I'm load - in' up my pis - tol. _

Bass Fig. 4

Asus4   A   Bsus4/A B/A G/A   N.C.   A5

I'm rid - in', I real - ly got a fist - ful. _

End Bass Fig. 4

6

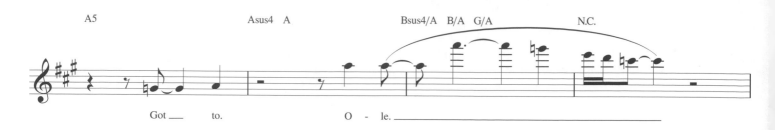

Got ___ to. O - le. ___

O - le. ___ Ooh, ___ ooh, ___ ooh. ___

O - le, ___ o - le, ___ o - le ___ who.

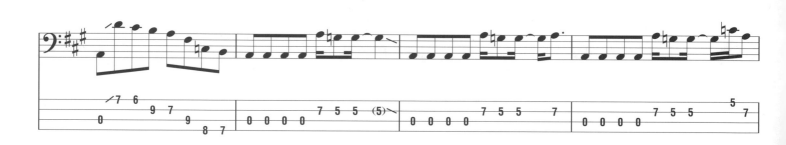

Get on! ___ Yeah! ___ Huh! ___

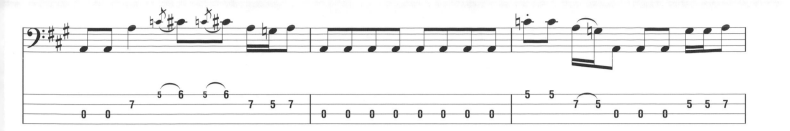

from *Toys in the Attic*

Big Ten Inch Record

Words and Music by Fred Weismantel

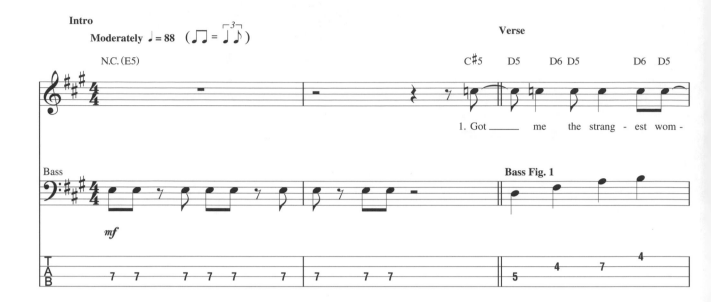

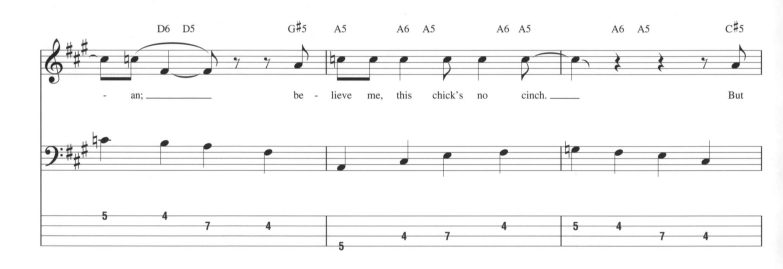

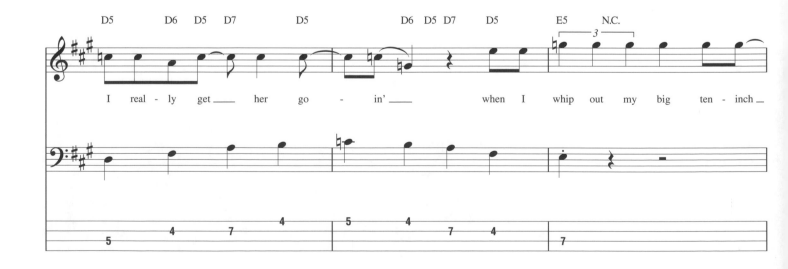

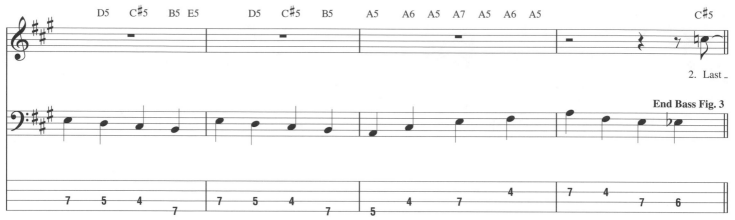

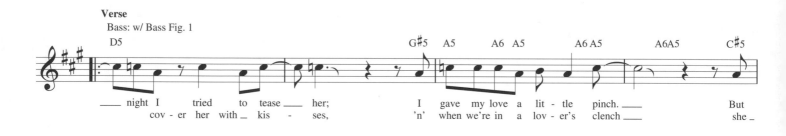

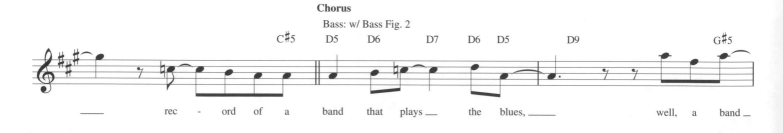

- ord of her fa- vor- ite blues. _____ 3. I, I, I'll _____ - ord of her fa- vor- ite blues. _____

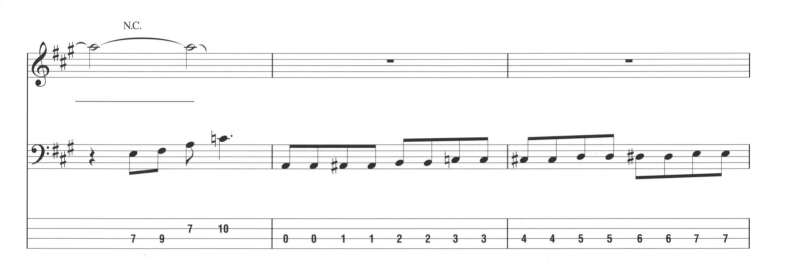

N.C.

Harmonica Solo
Bass: w/ Bass Fig. 3

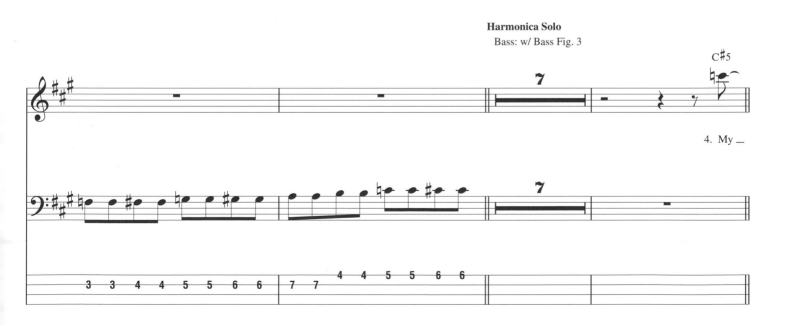

4. My _____

Verse
Bass: w/ Bass Fig. 1

___ girl don't ___ go for smok - in'; liq - our just makes her flinch.

___ Seems ___ she don't go for noth - in'; 'cept for my big ten - inch ___

Chorus
Bass: w/ Bass Fig. 2

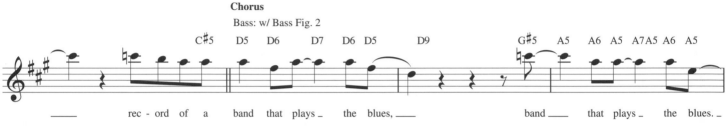

___ rec - ord of a band that plays _ the blues, ___ band ___ that plays _ the blues. _

___ She ___ just love ___ my big ___ ten - inch ___

Outro

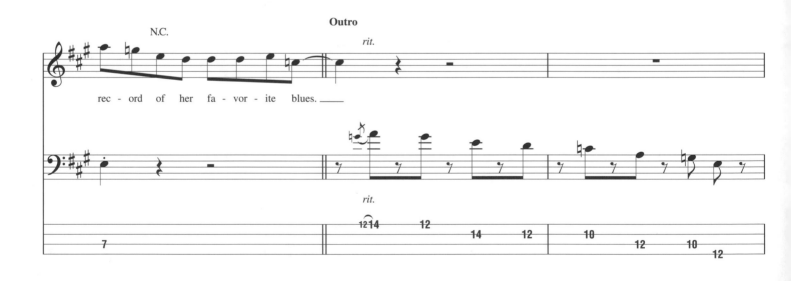

rec - ord of her fa - vor - ite blues. ___

Free time

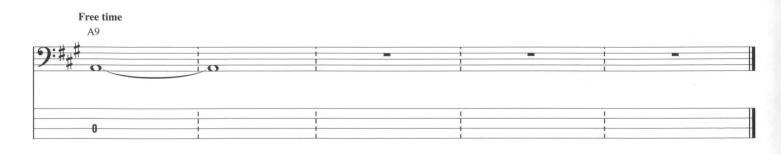

Come Together

Words and Music by John Lennon and Paul McCartney

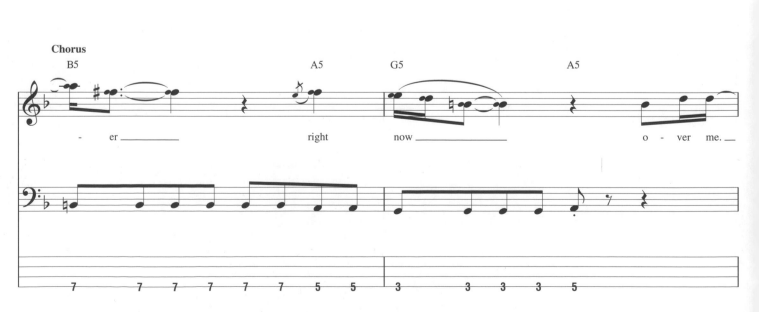

from *Big Ones*

Deuces Are Wild

Words and Music by Tyler/Vallance

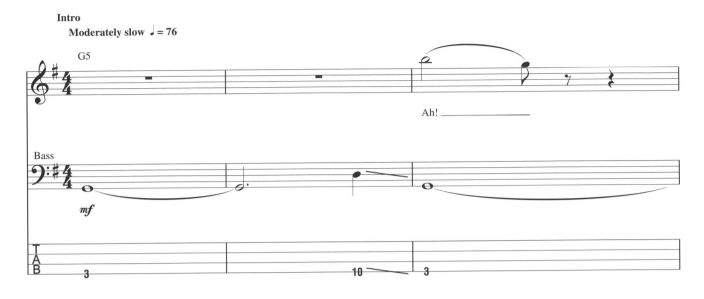

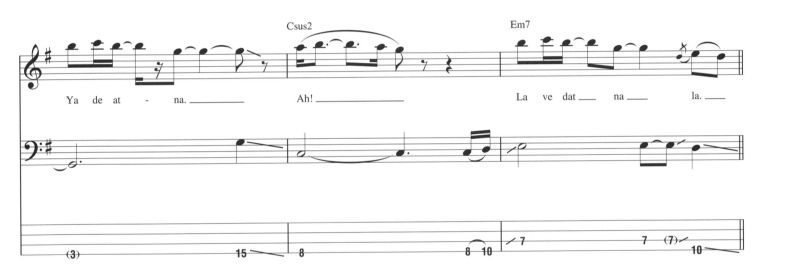

eyes. _____ They talk to me ___ and ___ seem to ___ hyp - no -
here. _____ Or some - where ___ else but ___ you been ___ al - ways

tize. _____ They say ___ the things ___ no - bod - y ___ dares to say.
near. _____ It's you that's in ___ my dreams ___ I'm ___ beg - gin' for.

_____ And I'm not a - bout ___ to ___ let you ___ fly a -
_____ But I woke up ___ when ___ some - one slammed _____ the door

1.

dou - ble shot of love is so fine. _____ Been lov - ing you since you was a child, _ girl, 'cause

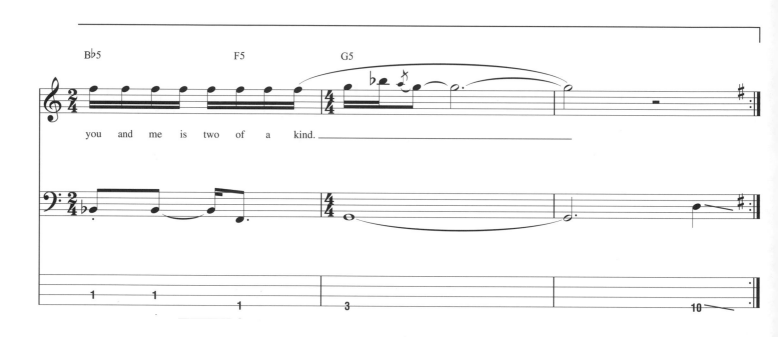

you and me is two of a kind. _____

2.

dou - ble shot of love is so fine. _____ I been lov - in' you since you was a child, _ girl, 'cause

Outro-Chorus

I love you 'cause your deuc - es are wild, __ girl, like a

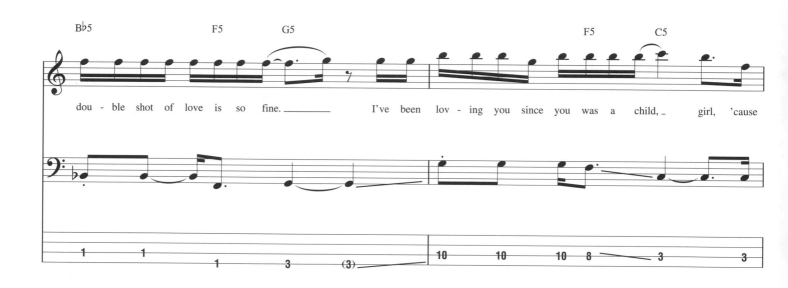

dou - ble shot of love is so fine. _____ I've been lov - ing you since you was a child, _ girl, 'cause

you and me are two of a kind. _____ I love you 'cause your deuc - es are wild, _ girl, yeah, a

dou - ble shot of love is so fine. _____ I been lov - ing you since you was a child, _ girl, 'cause

you and me is two of a kind. _____ I love you 'cause your deuc - es are wild, _ girl, you

know it, but I made up my mind. _____ I been lov - ing you since you was a child, _ girl, 'cause

you and me is two of a kind. _____ La la di la di do.

from *Aerosmith*

Dream On
Words and Music by Steven Tyler

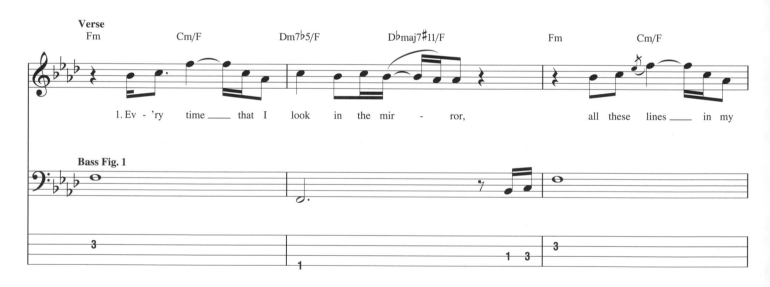

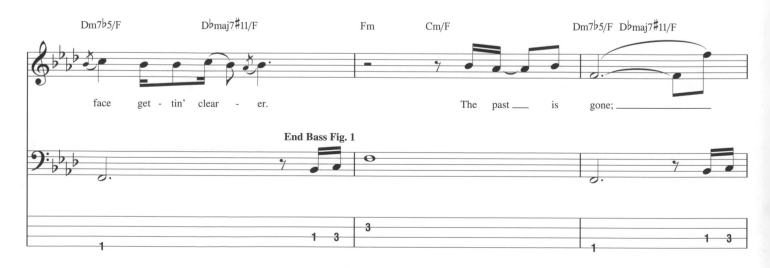

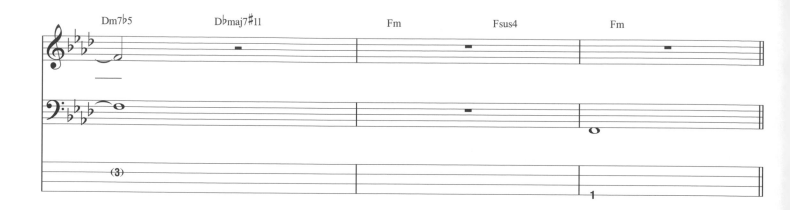

Verse
Bass: w/ Bass Fig. 1 (1 3/4 times)

2. Half __ my life's in book's writ - ten pa - ges, lived and learned from

fools and from sag - es. You know __ it's true _____ all these things _____

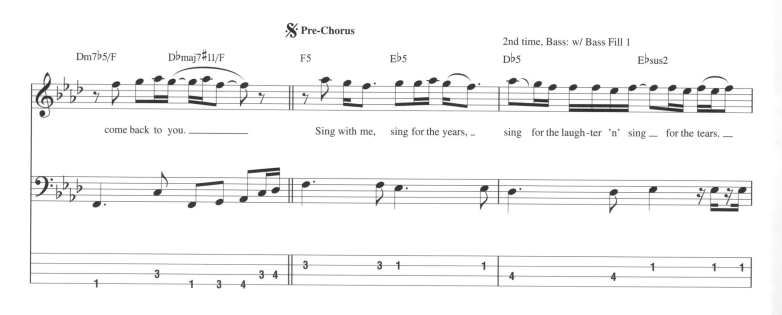

𝄋 Pre-Chorus

2nd time, Bass: w/ Bass Fill 1

come back to you. _____ Sing with me, sing for the years, _ sing for the laugh-ter 'n' sing _ for the tears. _

Bass Fill 1

28

Sing _ with me if it's just for to - day, _ may - be to - mor - row the good Lord will take you a - way. _

Well,

Sing it with me if it's just for to - day, __ may - be to - mor - row the good Lord will take you a - way.

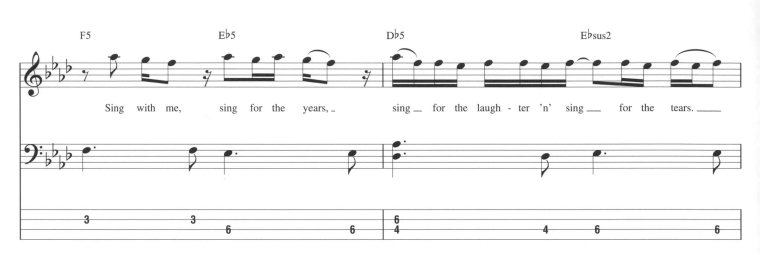

Sing with me, sing for the years, __ sing __ for the laugh - ter 'n' sing __ for the tears. __

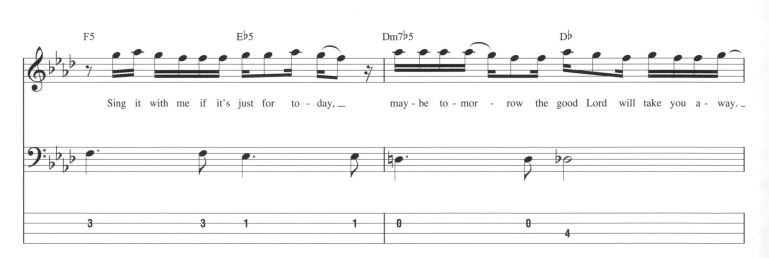

Sing it with me if it's just for to - day, __ may - be to - mor - row the good Lord will take you a - way. __

Outro *Fade out*

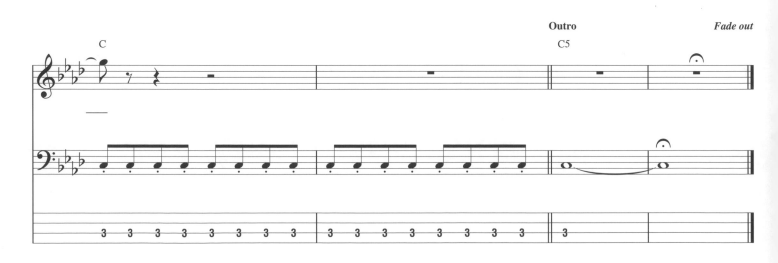

from *Permanent Vacation*

Dude (Looks Like a Lady)

Words and Music by Tyler/Perry/Child

5 String bass:
(low to high) B-E-A-D-G

Intro
Moderate Rock ♩ = 136

*Key signature denotes A Mixolydian.

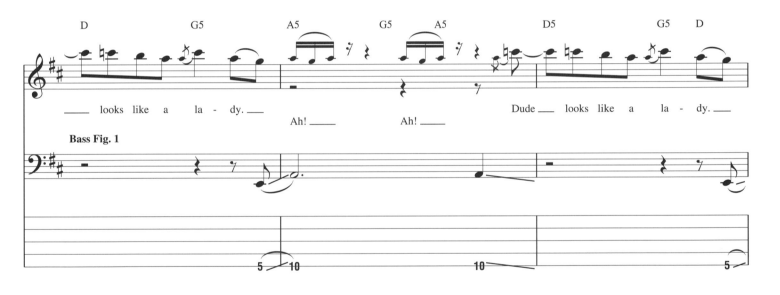

looks like a la - dy. _____

*Vocal tacet on repeat

1. Cruised in - to a bar on the shore. _____ Her pic - ture graced the grime on the door. _____
2. Back - stage we're hav - ing the time _____ of our lives _____ un - til _____ some - bod - y say, _____
nev - er judge a book by it's cov - er _____ or who your gon - na love by your lov

_____ She a long lost _____ love at first bite. _____ Ba - by may -
_____ "For - give me if I seem out of line." _____ Then she whipped _____
er. _____ Say _____ love put me wise _____ to her love in dis - guise. _____ She had the

- be you're wrong _____ but you know it's al - right. _____ That's right!
out her gun and tried to blow me a - way. _____
bod - y of a Ve - nus, Lord, i - mag - ine my sur - prise.

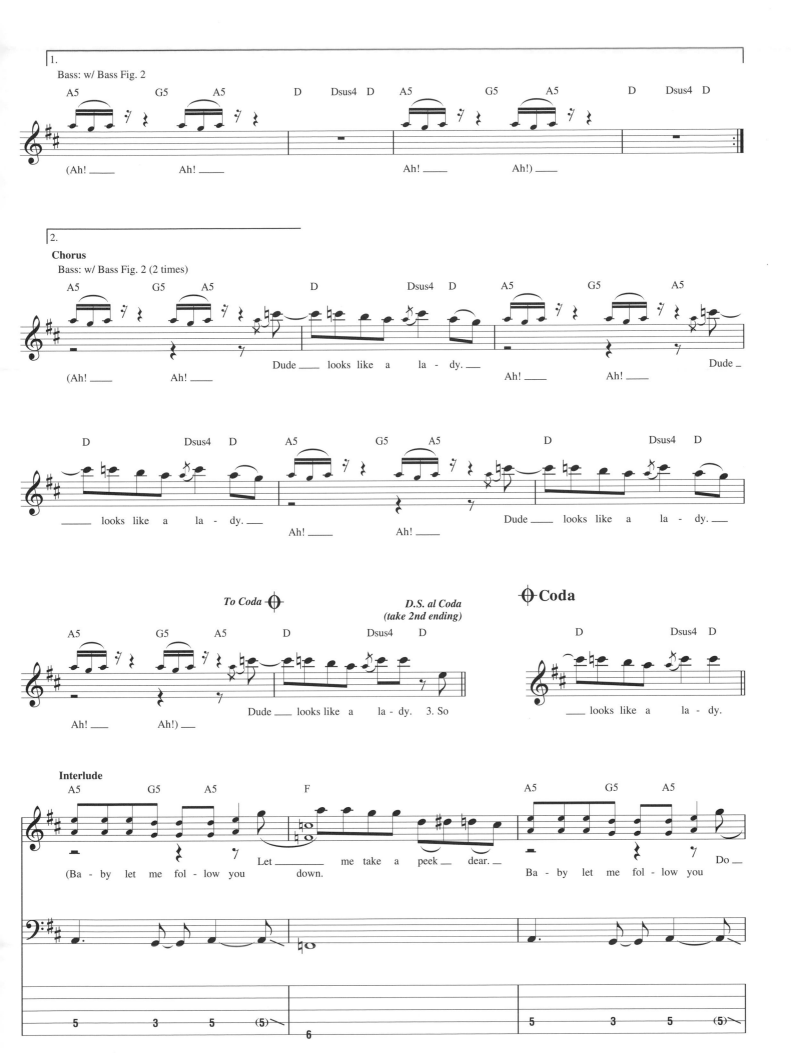

Ba - by let me fol - low you down.

down.

Turn _____ the oth - er cheek dear. _____

Ba - by let me fol - low you down.)

Do me, do me, do me, do _____ me. _____

Guitar Solo

Bass: w/ Bass Fig. 2 (4 times)

Play 4 times

Bridge

Ooh! What a fun - ky la - dy. _____ Oh, she

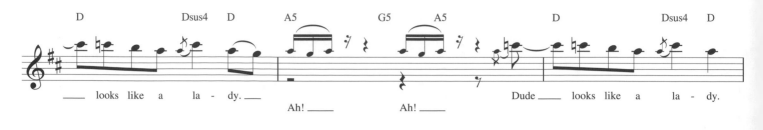

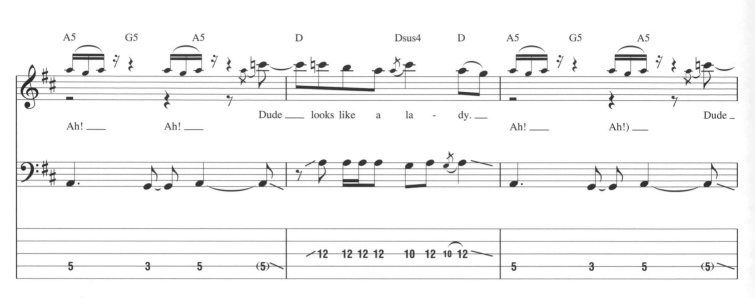

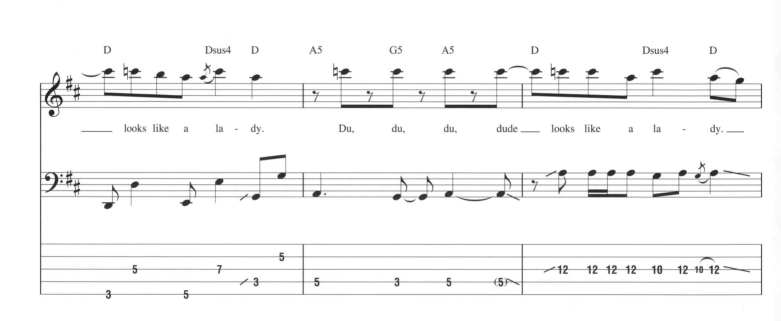

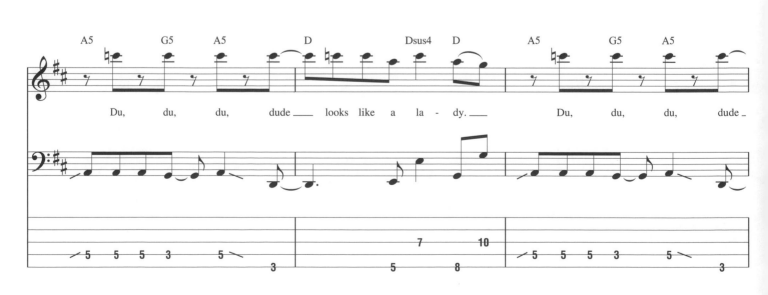

from *Big Ones*

Eat the Rich

Words and Music by Tyler/Perry/Vallance

1. Well, I

Verse

Bass: w/ Bass Fig. 1 (3 times)

N.C. (Em7)

woke up _____ this morn - ing on the wrong side of the bed. _____ And
called up my _____ head shrink - er and I told him what I'd done. _____ He said you'd

how I got to think - in' a - bout - a all those things you said. _____ A - bout
best go on _____ a di - et, yeah, I hope you have some fun. _____ And - a

or - di - nar - y peo - ple, and how they make you sick. _____ And if
don't go burst a bub - ble or the rich folks who get rude. _____ 'Cause you

call - in' names _____ kicks back on you, _____ then I hope this does the trick. Uh, 'cause I'm
won't get in no trou - ble when you eats that kind of food. Now they're

Pre-Chorus

E5   F#5   G5   A5

sick of your _____ com - plain - ing a - bout _____ how man - y bills. _____ And I'm
smok - ing up _____ their junk bonds, and then they go _____ get stiffed. _____ And they're
lieve in all _____ the good _____ things that mon - ey just _____ can't buy. _____ Uh, then

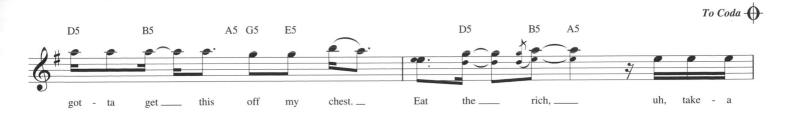

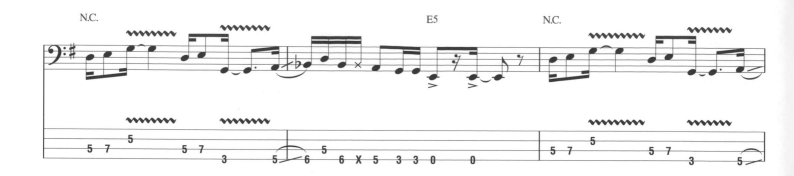

Guitar Solo

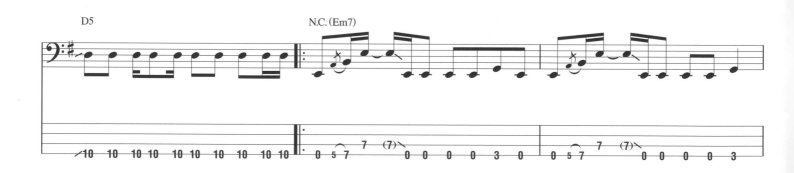

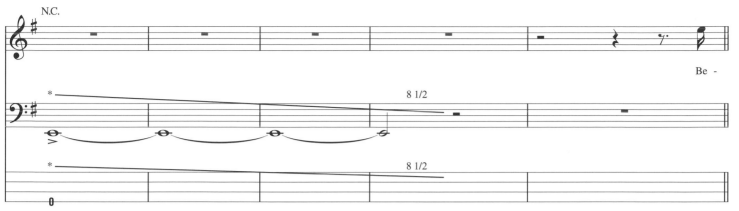

N.C.

Be -

*Pitch is lowered by turning tuning peg.

⊕ Coda

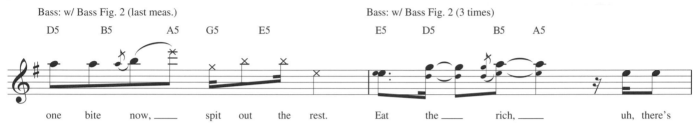

Bass: w/ Bass Fig. 2 (last meas.)

Bass: w/ Bass Fig. 2 (3 times)

| D5 | B5 | A5 | G5 | E5 | | E5 | D5 | B5 | A5 |

one bite now, ____ spit out the rest. Eat the ____ rich, ____ uh, there's

| D5 | B5 | A5 | G5 | E5 | | E5 | D5 | B5 | A5 | | D5 | B5 | A5 | G5 | E5 |

on - ly one thing that they're _ good for. Eat the ____ rich, _ uh, take - a one bite now, come back for more. _

| E5 | D5 | B5 | A5 | | D5 | B5 | A5 | G5 | E5 |

Eat the ____ rich, ____ uh, don't stop me now, ____ I'm go - in' cra - zy.

| E5 | D5 | B5 | A5 | | D5 | B5 | A5 | G5 | E5 |

Eat the ____ rich, ____ well, that's my i - dea ____ of a good time, ba - by!

1/4

from *Nine Lives*

Falling in Love (Is Hard on the Knees)

Words and Music by Tyler/Perry/Ballard

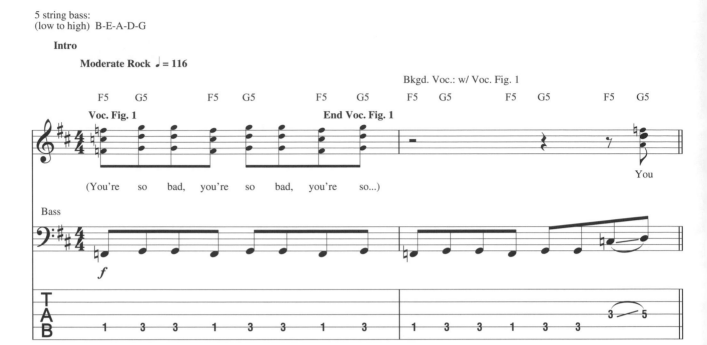

I thought ol' Cu - pid, he was tak - ing aim.
My fan - ta - size, it must be out of luck.
I was be - liev - er when you
My old li - bi - do has been

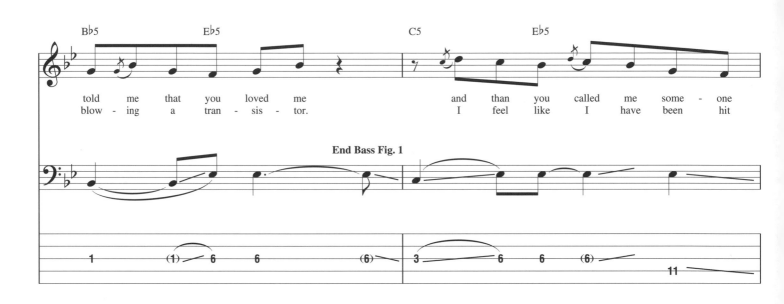

told me that you loved me and than you called me some - one
blow - ing a tran - sis - tor. I feel like I have been hit

End Bass Fig. 1

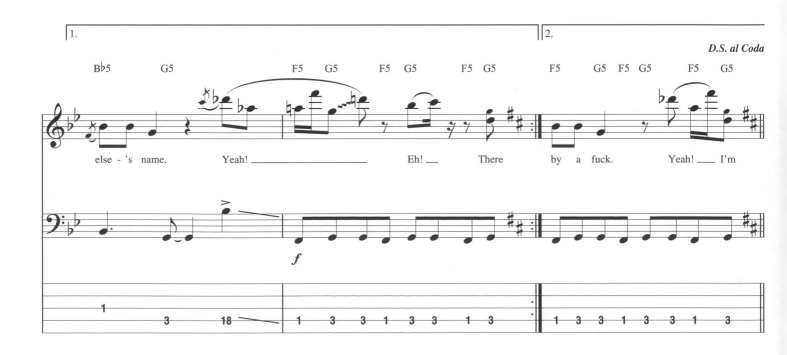

else - 's name. Yeah! Eh! There by a fuck. Yeah! I'm

D.S. al Coda

f

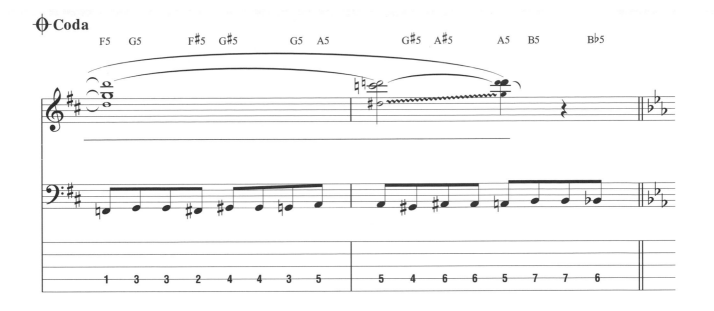

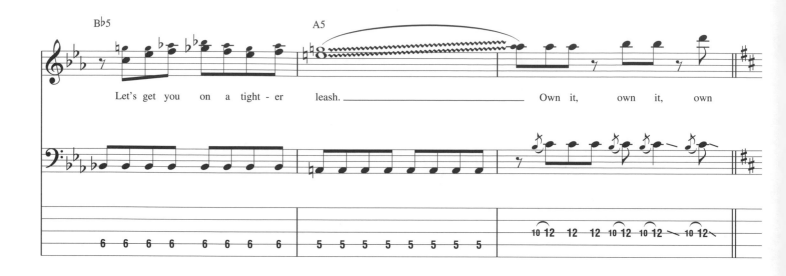

Let's get you on a tight-er leash. _____ Own it, own it, own

Guitar Solo

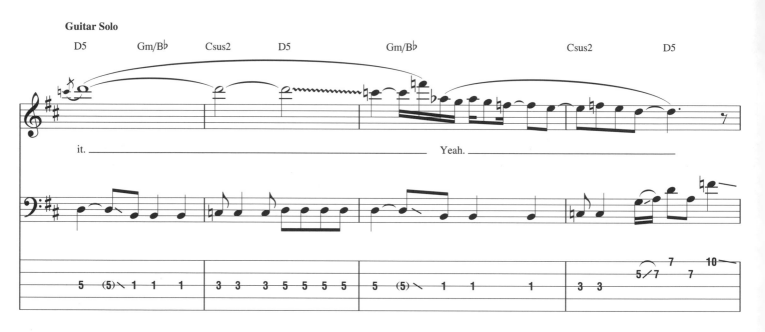

it. _____ Yeah.

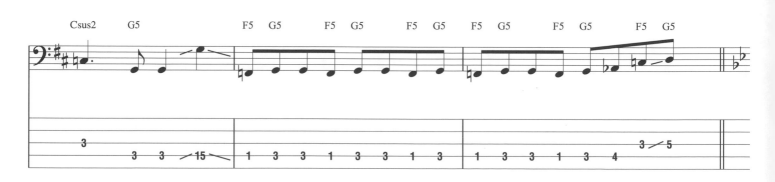

Verse

Bass: w/ Bass Fig. 1

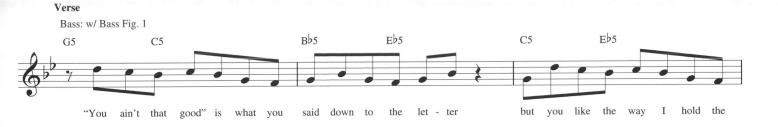

"You ain't that good" is what you said down to the let - ter   but you like the way I hold the

mi - cro - phone. (echo repeat)   Some - times I'm good, but when I'm   bad I'm e - ven bet - ter.

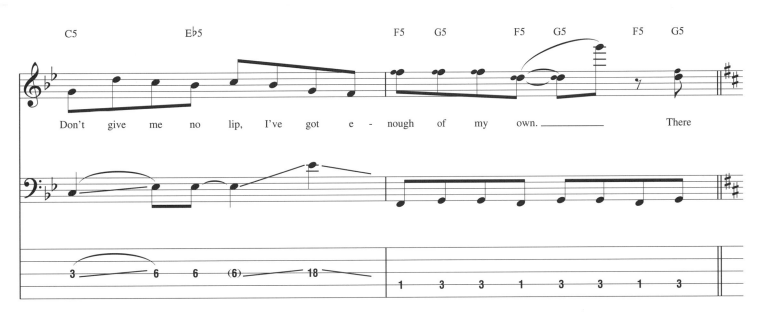

Don't give me no lip, I've got e - nough of my own. _____   There

Chorus

ain't gon - na be __ no more beg - gin' you please. __   You know what I want, _ and it ain't _

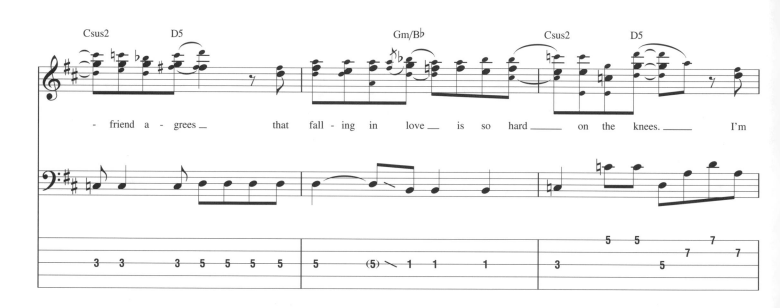

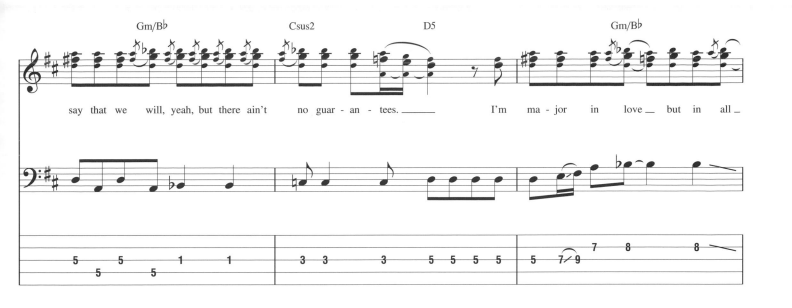

say that we will, yeah, but there ain't no guar - an - tees. _____ I'm ma - jor in love _____ but in all _____

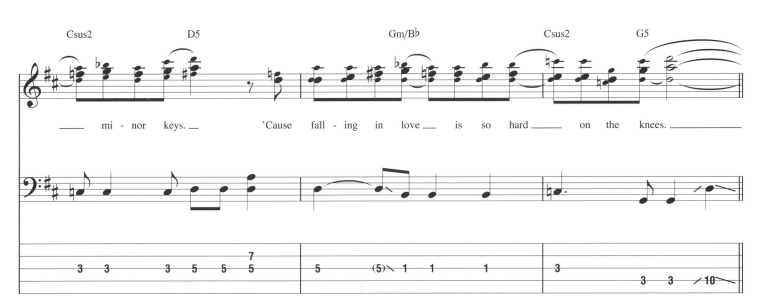

_____ mi - nor keys. _____ 'Cause fall - ing in love _____ is so hard _____ on the knees. _____

Outro

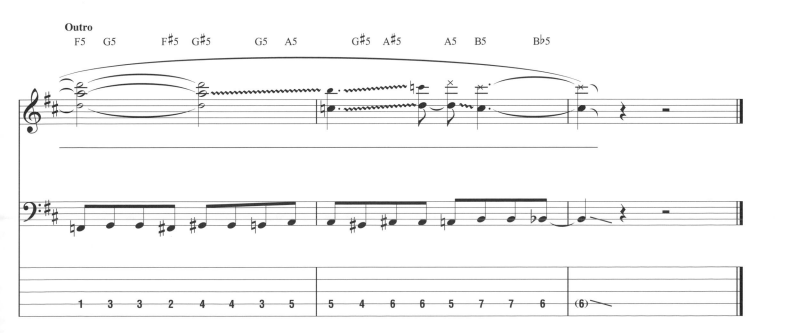

from *Pump*

Janie's Got a Gun

Words and Music by Tyler/Hamilton

5 String bass: tuned up 1/2 step:
(low to high) C-F-B♭-E♭-A♭

Intro

Moderately ♩ = 112

(Guitar & keyboards)

Dum, dum, __ dum, hon - ey what have you __ done? Dum, dum, __ dum it's the

*Chord symbols reflect overall harmony.

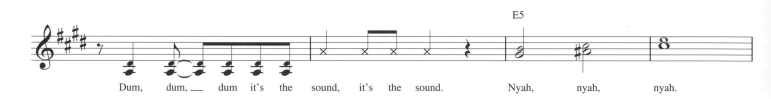

sound of my gun. Dum, dum, __ dum, hon - ey what have you __ done?

Dum, dum, __ dum it's the sound, it's the sound. Nyah, nyah, nyah.

Nyah, nyah, nyah. __ Nyah, nyah, nyah. Nyah, nyah, nyah.

Verse

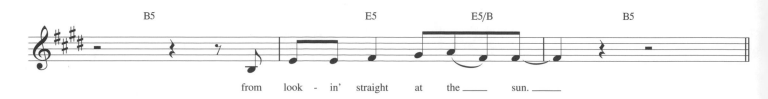

1. Jan - ie's got a __ gun. __

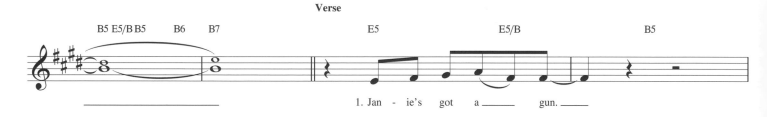

Jan - ie's got a __ gun. __ Her whole world's come un - done

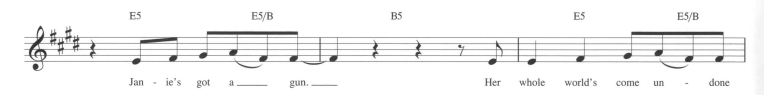

from look - in' straight at the __ sun.

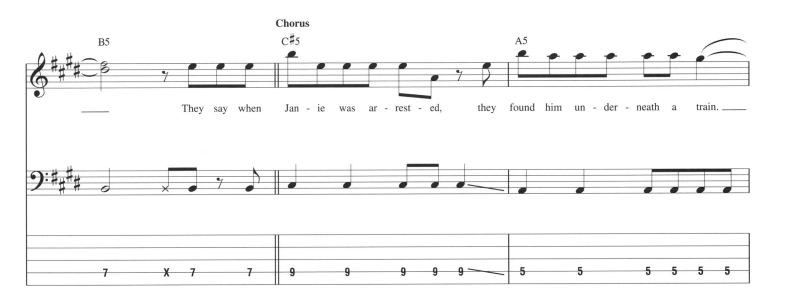

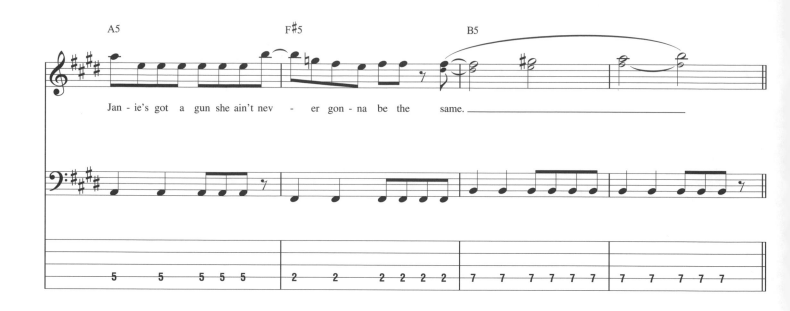

Jan - ie's got a gun she ain't nev - er gon - na be the same. _____

Verse

2. Jan - ie's got a _____ gun. _____ Jan - ie's got a _____ gun. _____

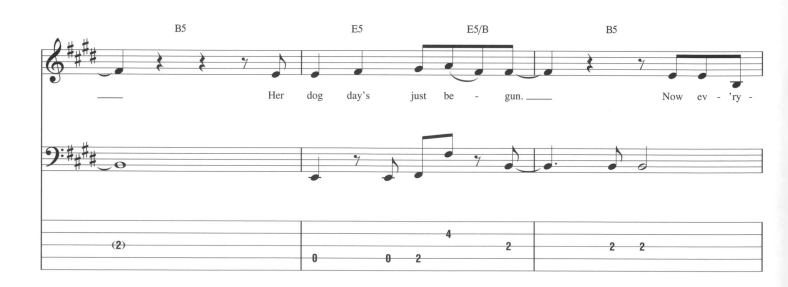

_____ Her dog day's just be - gun. _____ Now ev - 'ry -

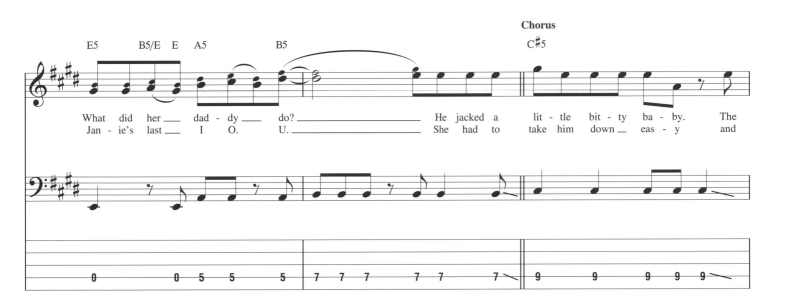

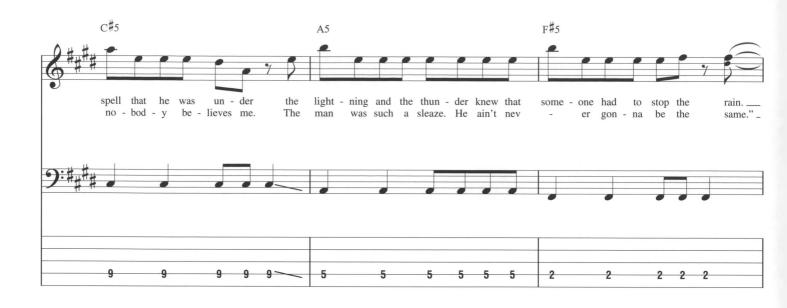

spell that he was un - der the light - ning and the thun - der knew that some - one had to stop the rain. __
no - bod - y be - lieves me. The man was such a sleaze. He ain't nev - er gon - na be the same." __

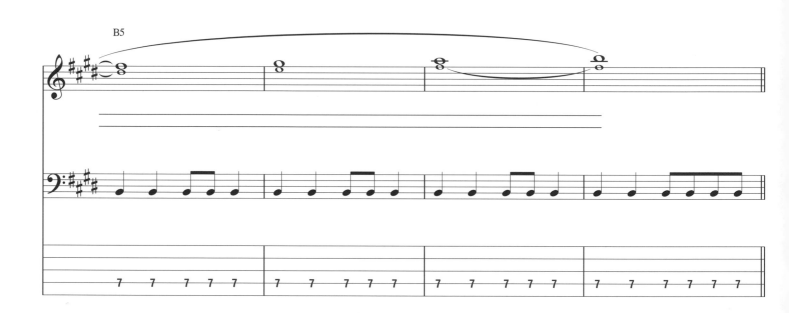

Bridge

Run a - way, run ____ a - way ____ from the pain, __ yeah, __ yeah, __

yeah, yeah, yeah. Run a - way, run _____ a - way _____ from the

pain, yeah, _____ yeah, yeah, _____ yeah, yeah, _____ yeah, yeah. _____ Run a - way,

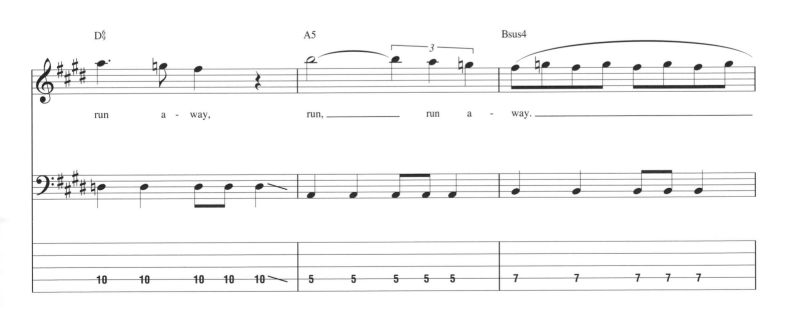

run a - way, run, _____ run a - way. _____

*Sing 1st time only.

Verse

3. Jan-ie's got a ___ gun. ___ Jan-ie's got a ___ gun. ___ Her

dog day's just be-gun. ___ Now ev-'ry-bod-y is on the ___ run. ___

Coda

Outro

Jan-ie's got a ___ gun. ___ Jan-ie's got a ___ gun. ___

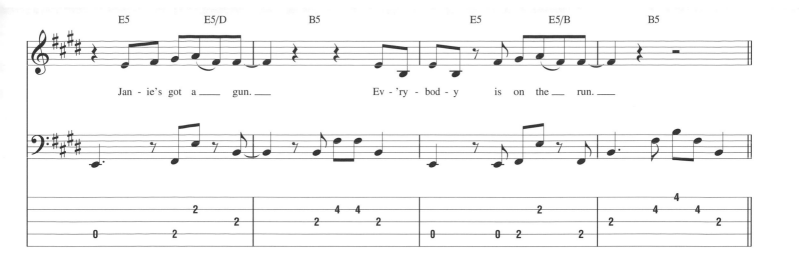

Love in an Elevator

Words and Music by Tyler/Perry

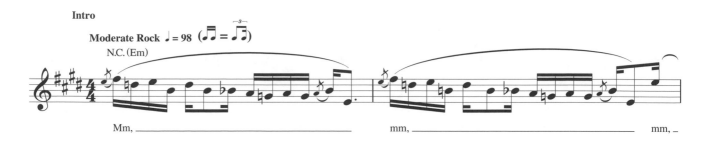

bet - tin' on the dice I'm — toss - in' / I'm gon - na have a fan - ta - sy. _____ But
said, "Can I see you — lat - er / and love you just a lit - tle more?" _____ I
(Whoa. _ / Whoa, _ yeah.) _

where am I gon - na look? _ / They tell me that love is blind. _ I
kind - a hope we get stuck _ / no - bod - y gets out a - live. ___ She said, I'll

real - ly need a girl like an o - pen book _ / to read be - tween _ the lines. _____
show you how to FAX in the mail - room / room hon - ey and have ya' home _ by five." _____

End Bass Fig. 1

Chorus

Love in an el - e - va - tor, _____ liv - in' it up ___ when I'm go - in' down. _____

Bass Fig. 2

1.

Love in an el - e - va - tor, _____ lov - in' it up ___ 'til I hit ___ the ground. _____

End Bass Fig. 2

2.

lov - in' it up ___ 'till I hit ___ the ground. _ In the air, _____ in the air, _____ hon - ey one _

el - e - va - tor.

Go - ing down.

Chorus
Bass: w/ Bass Fig. 2

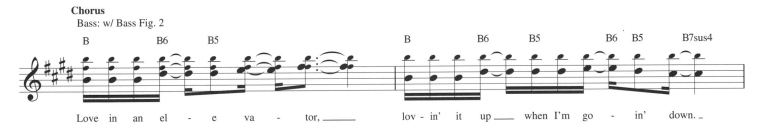

Love in an el - e - va - tor, _____ lov - in' it up ___ when I'm go - in' down. _

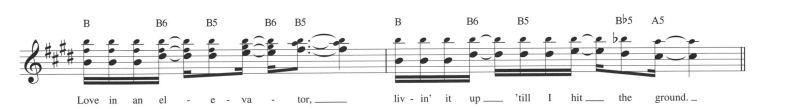

Love in an el - e - va - tor, _____ liv - in' it up ___ 'till I hit ___ the ground. _

Verse
Bass: w/ Bass Fig. 1

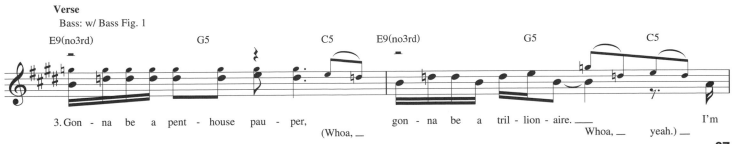

3. Gon - na be a pent - house pau - per, gon - na be a tril - lion - aire. ___ I'm
(Whoa, __ Whoa, __ yeah.) _

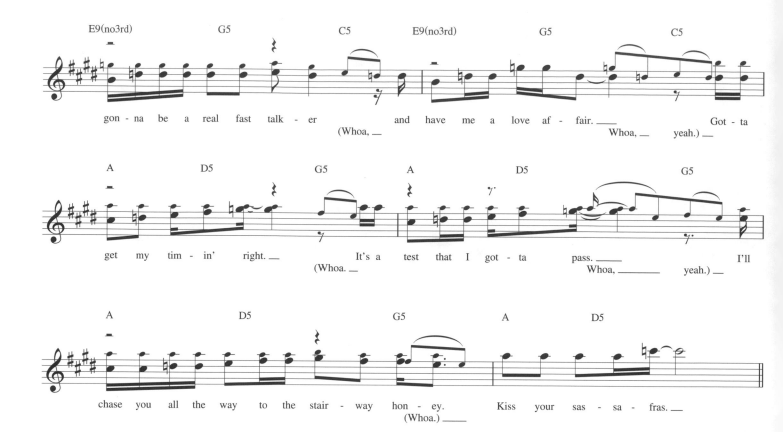

gon - na be a real fast talk - er and have me a love af - fair. ___ Got - ta
(Whoa, ___ Whoa, ___ yeah.) ___

get my tim - in' right. ___ It's a test that I got - ta pass. ___ I'll
(Whoa. ___ Whoa, _____ yeah.) ___

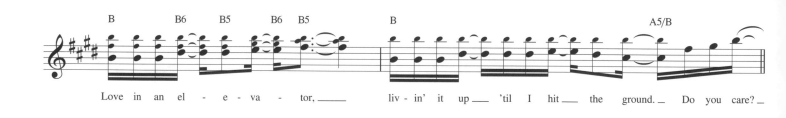

chase you all the way to the stair - way hon - ey. Kiss your sas - sa - fras. ___
(Whoa.) _____

Chorus

Bass: w/ Bass Fig. 2 (1st 2 meas.) (2 times)

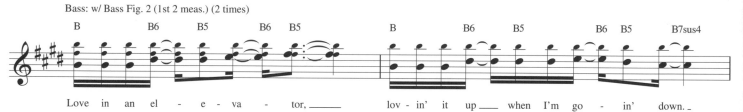

Love in an el - e - va - tor, _____ lov - in' it up ___ when I'm go - in' down. _

Love in an el - e - va - tor, _____ liv - in' it up ___ 'til I hit ___ the ground. _ Do you care?

Outro

___ ___ Do you care? ___ Hon - ey one ___ more time ___ now, it ___ ain't fair. ___

Love in an el - e - va - tor, _____ liv - in' it up ___ when I'm go - in' down. Do you care? _

_____ Do you care? _____ Hon - ey one ___ more time ___ now, it ___ ain't fair. _

Love in an el - e - va - tor, _____ liv - in' it up ___ when I'm go - in' down. _ In the air, _

in the air, _____ hon-ey, one __ more, one __ more, one __ more, one __ more.

Love in an el - e - va - tor, _____ liv-in' it up __ when I'm go - in' down. __ In the air, _

_____ in the air, _____ hon-ey, one __ more, one __ more, one __ more, one __ more.

Love in an el - e -va - tor, _____ liv-in' it up ___ when I'm go - in' down. ___ In the air, ___

_____ in the air, _____ hon - ey, one ___ more, one ___ more, one ___ more, one ___ more.

Love in an el - e -va - tor, _____

*Vocals fade out.

Love in an el - e - va - tor, _____ liv - in' it up ___ when I'm go - in' down. In the air, _

*Vocals fade in.

_____ in the air, _____ in the air, _____ in the air. _____

Fade out

Band tacet

Love in an el - e - va - tor, _____ lov - in' it up ___ when I'm go - in' down. _____

from *Aerosmith*

Mama Kin

Words and Music by Steven Tyler

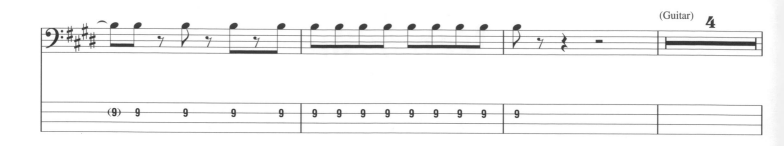

Verse

1. It ain't eas - y, liv - in' like a gyp - sy.___ Tell ___ ya, hon - ey, how I feel.___

I've been dream - in', float -

- in' down the stream and los - in' touch with all that's real.

Whole earth lov - er, keep - in' un - der cov - er, nev - er know - in' where you been.

Bass Fig. 1

drag - on. ___ You act like a per - pet - u - al drag. __

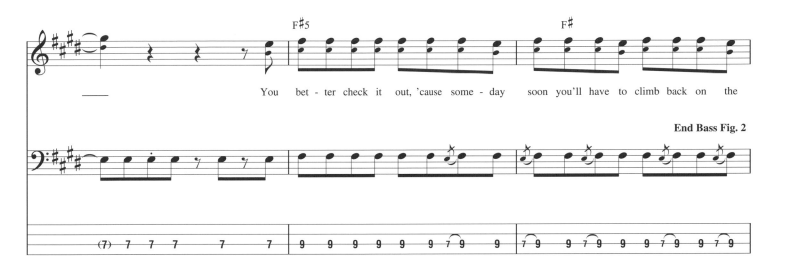

___ You bet - ter check it out, 'cause some - day soon you'll have to climb back on the

End Bass Fig. 2

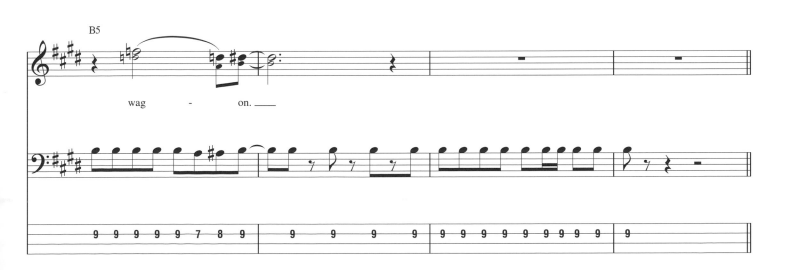

wag - on. ___

§ **Verse**

1st time, Bass tacet
2nd time, Bass: w/ Bass Fig. 1 (1st 2 meas.)   1st time, Bass: w/ Bass Fig. 1 (last 9 meas.)   2nd time, Bass: w/ Bass Fill 1

2., 3. It ain't eas-y liv-in' like you wan-na; mm, it's ___ so hard to find peace of mind, _

2nd time, Bass: w/ Bass Fig. 1 (last 6 meas.)

___ yes it is. The way I see it, you

got to say sheeit, _ but don't for-get to drop me a line. Said, you're

Pre-Chorus
Bass: w/ Bass Fig. 2

bald as an egg at eight-een, ___ and work-in' for your dad-dy's just a

___ drag. ___ You still stuff your mouth with them beans. _

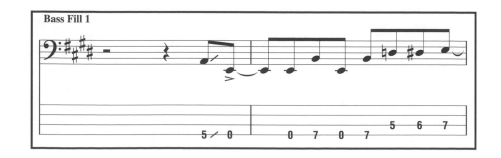

___ You bet-ter check it out, 'cause some-day soon you'll have to climb back on the

Bass Fill 1

Liv - in' out your fan - ta - sy, ___ sleep - in' late and smok - in' tea. ___

Interlude

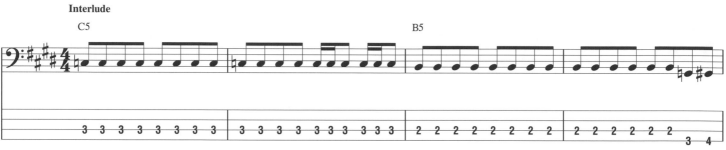

D.S. al Coda

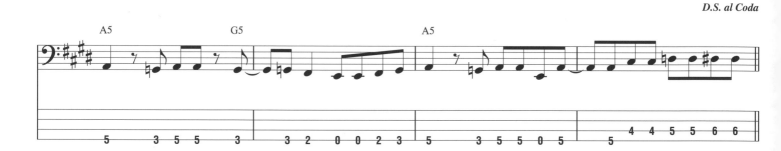

⊕ **Coda**

Slower ♩ = 216

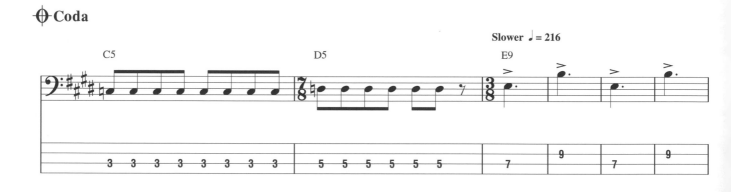

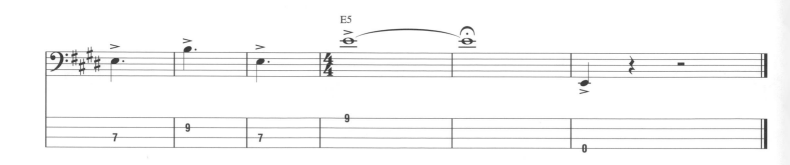

from *Greatest Hits*

Same Old Song & Dance

Words and Music by Steven Tyler and Joe Perry

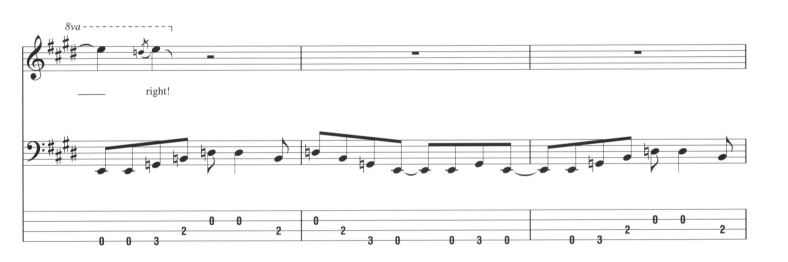

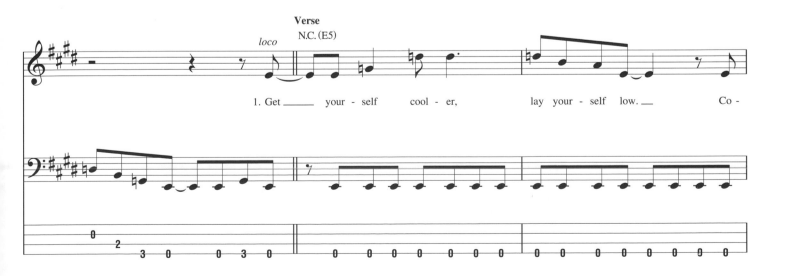

in-ci-den-tal mur-der with noth-in' to show. When the judge - - 's con-sti-pa-tion

goes to his head, and his wife's ag-gra-va-tion, you soon end up dead. It's the same

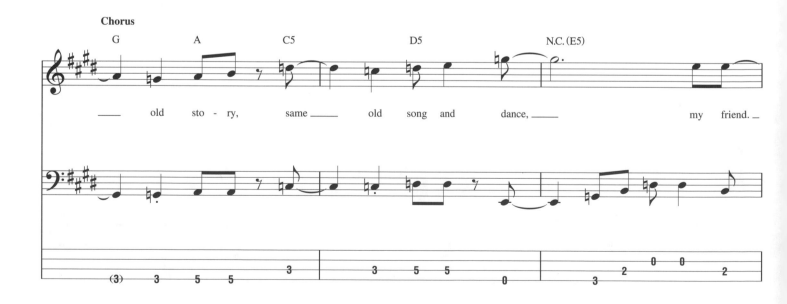

Chorus

old sto-ry, same old song and dance, my friend.

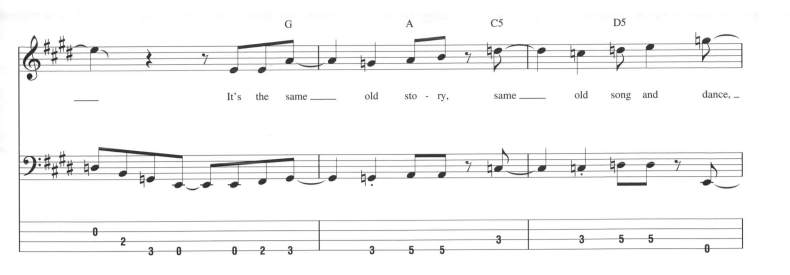

It's the same ___ old sto - ry, same ___ old song and dance, ___

Verse

___ my friend. ___ 2. Sha - dy look - in' los - er you
___ down and dir - ty from

played with my gun. ___ No smooth ___ face law - yer can get you un - done. ⎫
walk - in' the street ___ with your old ___ hur - dy gur - dy, no one to meet. ⎭ Say love ___

ain't the same on the south side o' town. You could look ___ but you ain't gon - na

Chorus

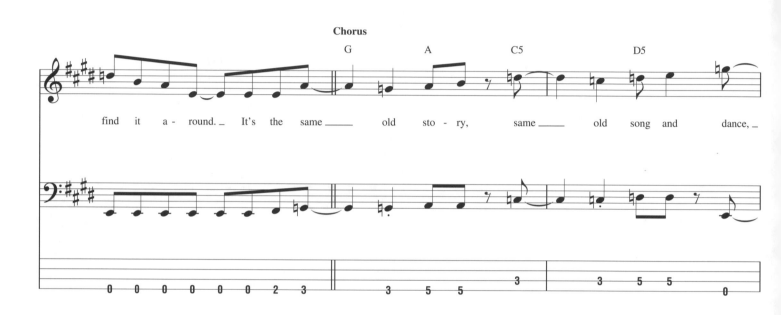

find it a - round. ___ It's the same ___ old sto - ry, same ___ old song and dance, __

___ my friend. ___ It's the same ___ old sto - ry, same __

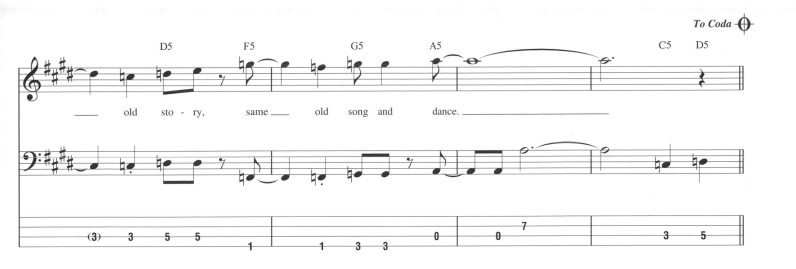

old sto - ry, same ____ old song and dance. _____

Guitar Solo

N.C. (E5)

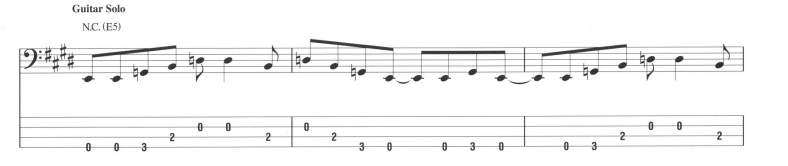

Bridge

*B5   A5   G5   A5   B5   A5   G5   A5   B5

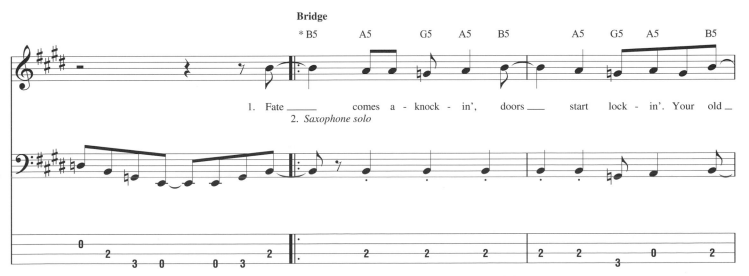

1. Fate _____ comes a - knock - in', doors ____ start lock - in'. Your old ___

2. *Saxophone solo*

*Chord symbols reflect guitar parts throughout Bridge.

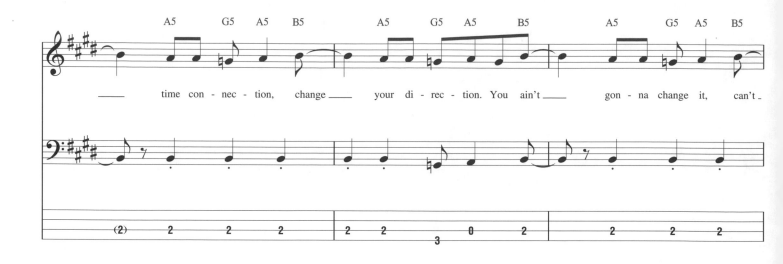

time con - nec - tion, change ___ your di - rec - tion. You ain't ___ gon - na change it, can't ___

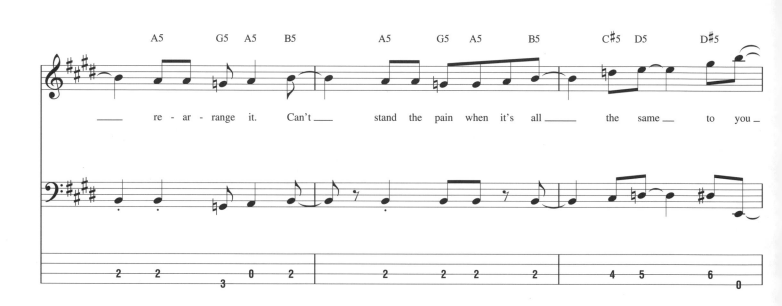

re - ar - range it. Can't ___ stand the pain when it's all ___ the same ___ to you ___

my friend. ___

3. When you're low___

⊕ Coda

from *Toys in the Attic*

Sweet Emotion

Words and Music by Steven Tyler and Tom Hamilton

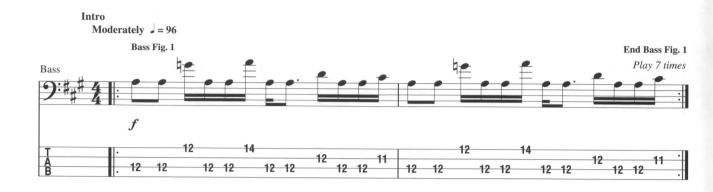

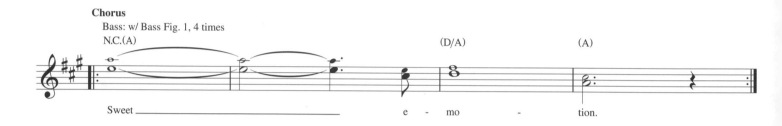

got good news, she's a real ____ good li - ar,   'cause my
talk - in' 'bout some - thin' you can sure un - der - stand,   'cause a

back - stage boo - gie set yo' pants on fire.
month on the road and I'll be eat - in' from your hand.

Interlude

Bass: w/ Bass Fig. 1, 4 times

Chorus

Sweet ____ e - mo - tion.   tion.   3. I

Coda

Outro

Play 12 times and fade

from *Toys in the Attic*

Toys in the Attic

Words and Music by Steven Tyler and Joe Perry

*Key signature denots E Mixolydian.

Verse

E5

1. Leav - in' the things ___ that are real _____ be - hind, ___

Bass Fig. 3

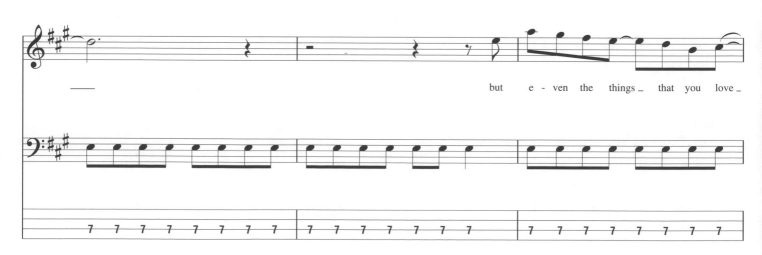

___ but e - ven the things ___ that you love ___

re - mind, ___ uh.

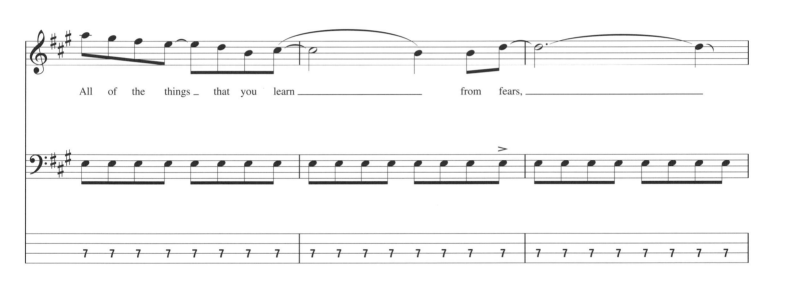

All of the things _ that you learn _____ from fears, _____

A5

noth - in' is left ___ but the years. _____

End Bass Fig. 3

5

toys ___ in the at - tic. Toys, toys, ___

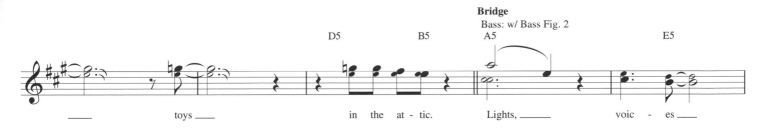

Bridge
Bass: w/ Bass Fig. 2

toys ___ in the at - tic. Lights, ___ voic - es ___

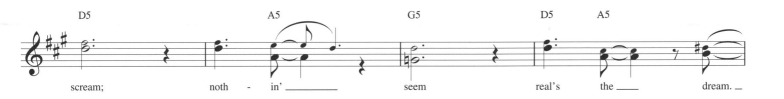

scream; noth - in' ___ seem real's the ___ dream. ___

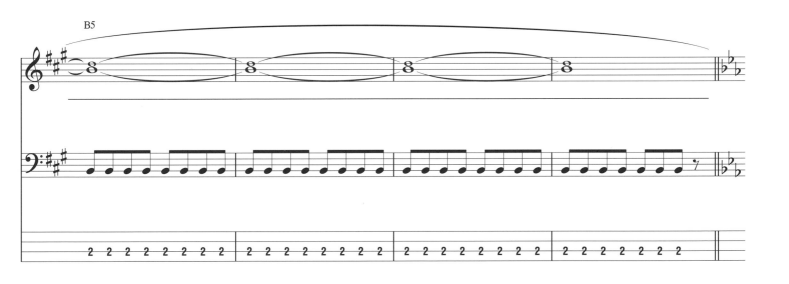

Guitar Solo

Bass: w/ Bass Fig. 5 (3 times)

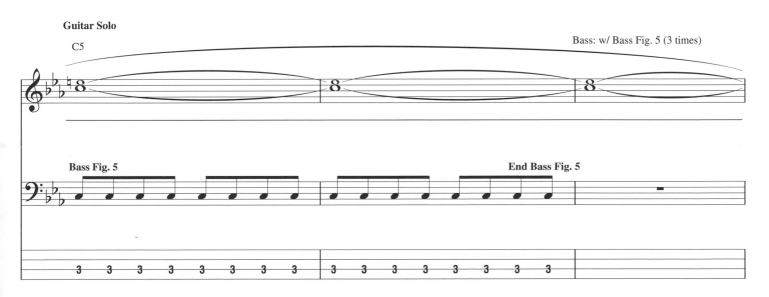

Bass Fig. 5   End Bass Fig. 5

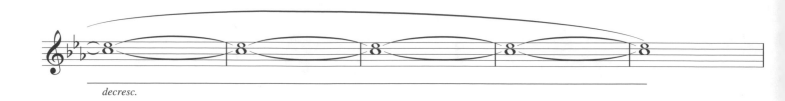

Verse

Bass: w/ Bass Fig. 3

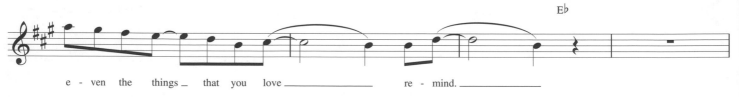

2. Leav - in' the things _ that are real _____ be - hind, _____ but

e - ven the things _ that you love _____ re - mind. _____

All of the things _ that you learn _____ from fears, _____

Bridge
Bass: w/ Bass Fig. 4

noth - in' is there __ but the years. __ Voic - es __ scream; noth - in' __

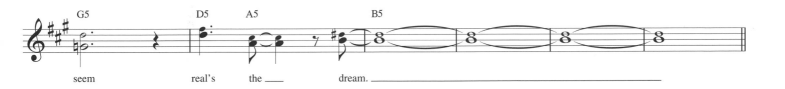

seem real's the __ dream. __

Outro-Chorus
Bass: w/ Bass Fig. 1 (1st 4 meas.) (4 times)

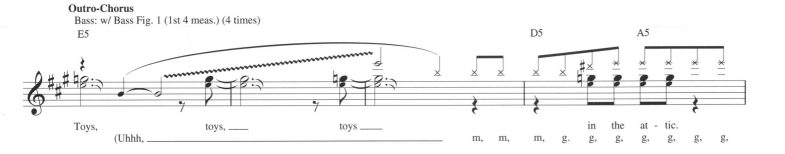

Toys, toys, __ toys __ in the at - tic.
(Uhhh, __ m, m, m, g. g, g, g, g, g, g,

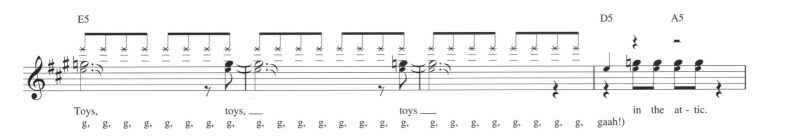

Toys, toys, __ toys __ in the at - tic.
g, g, g, g, g, g, g, g, g, g, g, g, g, g, g, g, g, g, g, g, g, g, g, g, gaah!)

Toys, toys, __ toys __ were in the at - tic.

Toys, toys, __ toys __ in the at - tic.

Begin fade   ***Play 3 times and fade***
Bass: w/ Bass Fig. 1 (1st 4 meas.) (till fade)

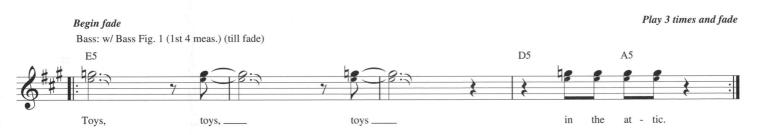

Toys, toys, __ toys __ in the at - tic.

from *Get Your Wings*
Train Kept a-Rollin'
Words and Music by Tiny Bradshaw, Lois Mann and Howie Kay

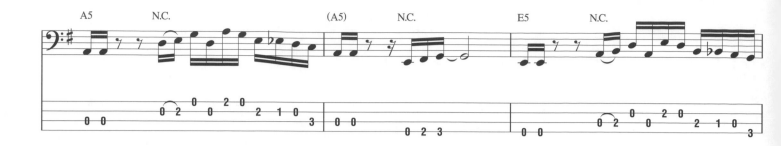

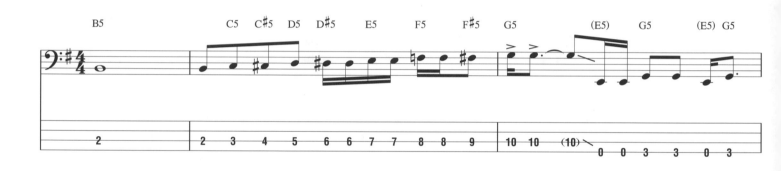

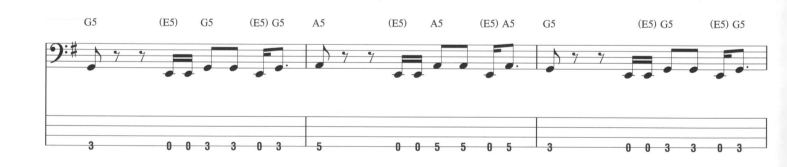

Interlude
Faster ♩ = 198

Bass tacet
(Snare drum & guitar)

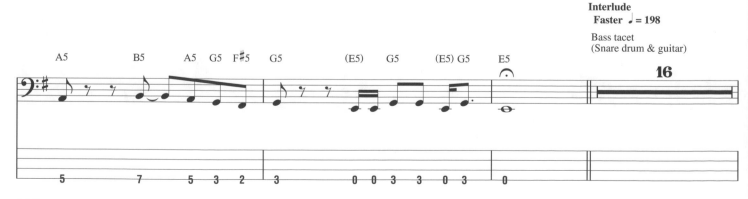

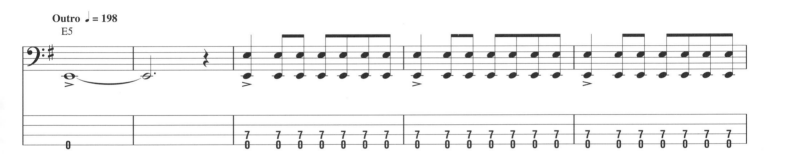

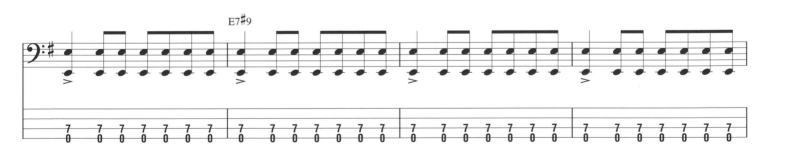

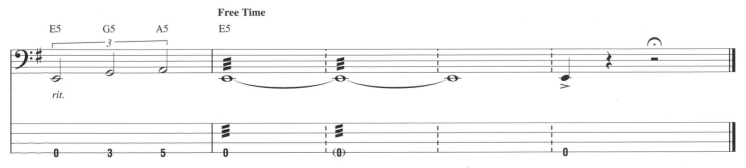

Walk This Way

Words and Music by Steven Tyler and Joe Perry

Intro

Moderate Rock ♩ = 120

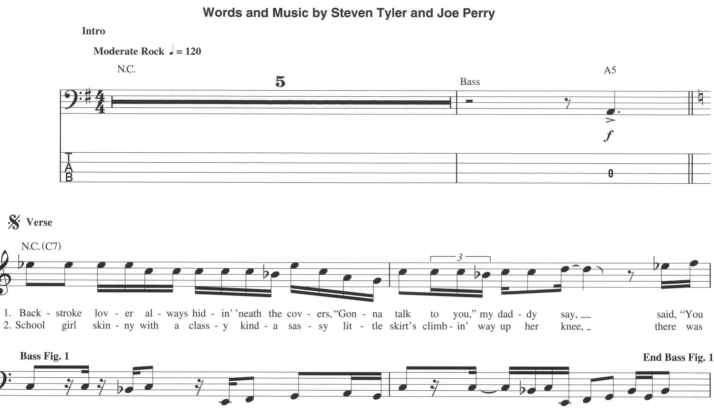

% Verse

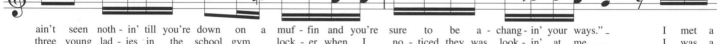

1. Back - stroke lov - er al - ways hid - in' 'neath the cov - ers, "Gon - na talk to you," my dad - dy say, __ said, "You
2. School girl skin - ny with a class - y kind - a sas - sy lit - tle skirt's climb - in' way up her knee, __ there was

Bass Fig. 1   **End Bass Fig. 1**

Bass: w/ Bass Fig. 1 (2 times)

ain't seen noth - in' till you're down on a muf - fin and you're sure to be a - chang - in' your ways." __ I met a
three young lad - ies in the school gym lock - er when I no - ticed they was look - in' at me. __ I was a

cheer - lead - er, was a real young bleed - er all the times I could rem - i - nisce, __ 'cause the
high school los - er, nev - er made it with a la - dy 'til the boys told me some - thin' I missed, __ then my

best things in lov - in' with a sis - ter and a cou - sin on - ly start - ed with a lit - tle kiss, __ a - like this!
next door neigh - bor with a daugh - ter had a fav - or so I gave her just a lit - tle kiss __ a - like this!

Interlude

N.C. (E5)

Bass Fig. 2

A5

End Bass Fig. 2

Verse

Bass: w/ Bass Fig. 1 (3 times)

N.C. (C7)

2., 4. See - saw swing - in' with the boys in the school and your feet fly - in' up in the air, ___ I sing,

"Hey did - dle did - dle" with your kit - ty in the mid - dle of the swing like you did - n't care. ___ So I

*

took a big chance at the high school dance with a mis - sy who was read - y to play, ___ was a

*Sing harmony 1st time only.

me she was fool - in' 'cause she knew what she was do - in' { and I know'd love was here to stay ___ when she told me to...

{ when she told me how to walk this way. ___ She told ___ me to...

Coda

C7 — F7

walk this ___ way, ___ talk this ___ way.) ___ Uh, just gim-me a kiss. ___

Guitar Solo

N.C. (C7)

A5

Like this!

Play 12 times and fade

N.C.

Bass Notation Legend

Bass music can be notated two different ways: on a *musical staff*, and in *tablature*.

THE MUSICAL STAFF shows pitches and rhythms and is divided by bar lines into measures. Pitches are named after the first seven letters of the alphabet.

TABLATURE graphically represents the bass fingerboard. Each horizontal line represents a string, and each number represents a fret.

3rd string, open   2nd string, 2nd fret   1st & 2nd strings open, played together

HAMMER-ON: Strike the first (lower) note with one finger, then sound the higher note (on the same string) with another finger by fretting it without picking.

PULL-OFF: Place both fingers on the notes to be sounded. Strike the first note and without picking, pull the finger off to sound the second (lower) note.

LEGATO SLIDE: Strike the first note and then slide the same fret-hand finger up or down to the second note. The second note is not struck.

SHIFT SLIDE: Same as legato slide, except the second note is struck.

TRILL: Very rapidly alternate between the notes indicated by continuously hammering on and pulling off.

TREMOLO PICKING: The note is picked as rapidly and continuously as possible.

VIBRATO: The string is vibrated by rapidly bending and releasing the note with the fretting hand.

SHAKE: Using one finger, rapidly alternate between two notes on one string by sliding either a half-step above or below.

NATURAL HARMONIC: Strike the note while the fret hand lightly touches the string directly over the fret indicated.

MUFFLED STRINGS: A percussive sound is produced by laying the fret hand across the string(s) without depressing them and striking them with the pick hand.

BEND: Strike the note and bend up the interval shown.

BEND AND RELEASE: Strike the note and bend up as indicated, then release back to the original note. Only the first note is struck.

RIGHT-HAND TAP: Hammer ("tap") the fret indicated with the "pick-hand" index or middle finger and pull off to the note fretted by the fret hand.

LEFT-HAND TAP: Hammer ("tap") the fret indicated with the "fret-hand" index or middle finger.

SLAP: Strike ("slap") string with right-hand thumb.

POP: Snap ("pop") string with right-hand index or middle finger.

Additional Musical Definitions

 (accent)
- Accentuate note (play it louder)

 (accent)
- Accentuate note with great intensity

 (staccato)
- Play the note short

⊓
- Downstroke

∨
- Upstroke

D.S. al Coda
- Go back to the sign (𝄋), then play until the measure marked "***To Coda***," then skip to the section labelled "**Coda**."

D.C. al Fine
- Go back to the beginning of the song and play until the measure marked "***Fine***" (end).

Bass Fig.
- Label used to recall a recurring pattern.

Fill
- Label used to identify a brief pattern which is to be inserted into the arrangement.

tacet
- Instrument is silent (drops out).

- Repeat measures between signs.

| 1. | 2. |
- When a repeated section has different endings, play the first ending only the first time and the second ending only the second time.

NOTE: Tablature numbers in parentheses mean:
1. The note is being sustained over a system (note in standard notation is tied), or
2. The note is sustained, but a new articulation (such as a hammer-on, pull-off, slide or vibrato begins), or
3. The note is a barely audible "ghost" note (note in standard notation is also in parentheses).

BASS RECORDED VERSIONS

Bass Recorded Versions® feature authentic transcriptions written in standard notation and tablature for bass guitar. This series features complete bass lines from the classics to contemporary superstars.

   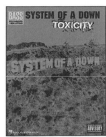 

25 All-Time Rock Bass Classics
00690445 / $14.95

25 Essential Rock Bass Classics
00690210 / $14.95

Bass Tab 1990-1999
00690400 / $16.95

Bass Tab 1999-2000
00690404 / $14.95

Bass Tab 2000
00690434 / $14.95

Bass Tab 2001
00690522 / $14.95

Bass Tab White Pages
00690508 / $29.95

The Beatles Bass Lines
00690170 / $12.95

The Beatles 1962-1966
00690556 / $17.95

The Beatles 1966-1970
00690557 / $16.95

Best Bass Rock Hits
00694803 / $12.95

Black Sabbath – We Sold Our Soul For Rock 'N' Roll
00660116 / $17.95

The Best of Blink 182
00690549 / $17.95

Blues Bass Classics
00690291 / $14.95

The Best of Eric Clapton
00660187 / $16.95

Stanley Clarke Collection
00672307 / $19.95

Jimi Hendrix – Are You Experienced?
00690371 / $14.95

Jimi Hendrix – Axis Bold As Love
00690373 / $14.95

Jimi Hendrix – Electric Ladyland
00690375 / $14.95

The Buddy Holly Bass Book
00660132 / $12.95

Incubus – Morning View
00690639 / $17.95

Bob Marley Bass Collection
00690568 / $17.95

Motown Bass Classics
00690253 / $14.95

Nirvana Bass Collection
00690066 / $19.95

Jaco Pastorius – Greatest Jazz Fusion Bass Player
00690421 / $17.95

The Essential Jaco Pastorius
00690420 / $17.95

Pearl Jam – Ten
00694882 / $14.95

Pink Floyd – Dark Side of the Moon
00660172 / $14.95

The Best of Police
00660207 / $14.95

Queen – The Bass Collection
00690065 / $17.95

Rage Against the Machine
00690248 / $16.95

Rage Against the Machine – Evil Empire
00690249 / $14.95

Red Hot Chili Peppers – Blood Sugar Sex Magik
00690064 / $19.95

Red Hot Chili Peppers - By the Way
00690585 / $19.95

Red Hot Chili Peppers – Californication
00690390 / $19.95

Red Hot Chili Peppers – Greatest Hits
00690675 / $17.95

Red Hot Chili Peppers – One Hot Minute
00690091 / $18.95

Rock Bass Bible
00690446 / $18.95

Rolling Stones
00690256 / $14.95

System of a Down – Toxicity
00690592 / $19.95

Stevie Ray Vaughan – In Step
00694777 / $14.95

Stevie Ray Vaughan – Lightnin' Blues 1983-1987
00694778 / $19.95

FOR MORE INFORMATION, SEE YOUR LOCAL MUSIC DEALER, OR WRITE TO:

HAL•LEONARD®
CORPORATION

7777 W. BLUEMOUND RD. P.O. BOX 13819 MILWAUKEE, WI 53213

Visit Hal Leonard Online at
www.halleonard.com

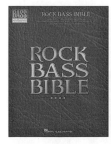

Hal•Leonard BASS PLAY•ALONG

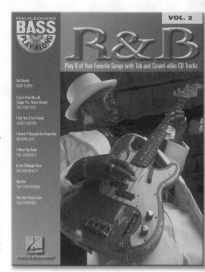

The Bass Play-Along Series will help you play your favorite songs quickly and easily! Just follow the tab, listen to the CD to hear how the bass should sound, and then play along using the separate backing tracks. The melody and lyrics are also included in the book in case you want to sing, or to simply help you follow along. The audio CD is playable on any CD player. For PC and Mac computer users, the CD is enhanced so you can adjust the recording to any tempo without changing pitch!

Rock VOLUME 1
Songs: Another One Bites the Dust • Badge • Brown Eyed Girl • Come Together • The Joker • Low Rider • Money • Sweet Emotion.
00699674 Book/CD Pack....................................$12.95

R&B VOLUME 2
Songs: Get Ready • I Can't Help Myself (Sugar Pie, Honey Bunch) • I Got You (I Feel Good) • I Heard It Through the Grapevine • I Want You Back • In the Midnight Hour • My Girl • You Can't Hurry Love.
00699675 Book/CD Pack....................................$12.95

Pop/Rock VOLUME 3
Songs: Crazy Little Thing Called Love • Crocodile Rock • Maneater • My Life • No Reply at All • Peg • Message in a Bottle • Suffragette City.
00699677 Book/CD Pack....................................$12.95

'90s Rock VOLUME 4
Songs: All I Wanna Do • Fly Away • Give It Away • Hard to Handle • Jeremy • Know Your Enemy • Spiderwebs • You Oughta Know.
00699679 Book/CD Pack....................................$12.95

Funk VOLUME 5
Songs: Brick House • Cissy Strut • Get Off • Get Up (I Feel Like Being) a Sex Machine • Higher Ground • Le Freak • Pick up the Pieces • Super Freak.
00699680 Book/CD Pack....................................$12.95

Classic Rock VOLUME 6
Songs: Free Ride • Funk #49 • Gimme Three Steps • Green-Eyed Lady • Radar Love • Werewolves of London • White Room • Won't Get Fooled Again.
00699678 Book/CD Pack....................................$12.95

Hard Rock VOLUME 7
Songs: Crazy Train • Detroit Rock City • Iron Man • Livin' on a Prayer • Living After Midnight • Peace Sells • Smoke on the Water • The Trooper.
00699676 Book/CD Pack....................................$12.95

Prices, contents and availability subject to change without notice.

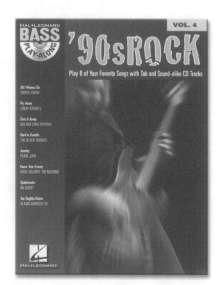

FOR MORE INFORMATION,
SEE YOUR LOCAL MUSIC DEALER,
OR WRITE TO:

HAL•LEONARD®
CORPORATION
7777 W. BLUEMOUND RD. P.O. BOX 13819
MILWAUKEE, WISCONSIN 53213
Visit Hal Leonard Online at **www.halleonard.com**